SOME MAJOR EVENTS IN WORLD WAR II

THE EUROPEAN THEATER

1939 SEPTEMBER—Germany invades Poland; Great Britain, France, Australia, & New Zealand declare war on Germany; Battle of the Atlantic begins. NOVEMBER—Russia invades Finland.

1940 APRIL—Germany invades Denmark & Norway. MAY—Germany invades Belgium, Luxembourg, & The Netherlands; British forces retreat to Dunkirk and escape to England. JUNE—Italy declares war on Britain & France; France surrenders to Germany. JULY—Battle of Britain begins. SEPTEMBER—Italy invades Egypt; Germany, Italy, & Japan form the Axis countries. OCTOBER—Italy invades Greece. NOVEMBER—Battle of Britain over. DECEMBER—Britain attacks Italy in North Africa.

1941 JANUARY—Allies take Tobruk. FEBRUARY—Rommel arrives at Tripoli. APRIL—Germany invades Greece & Yugoslavia. JUNE—Allies are in Syria; Germany invades Russia. JULY—Russia joins Allies. AUGUST—Germans capture Kiev. OCTOBER—Germany reaches Moscow. DECEMBER—Germans retreat from Moscow; Japan attacks Pearl Harbor; United States enters war against Axis nations.

1942 MAY—first British bomber attack on Cologne. JUNE—Germans take Tobruk. SEPTEMBER—Battle of Stalingrad begins. OCTOBER—Battle of El Alamein begins. NOVEMBER—Allies recapture Tobruk; Russians counterattack at Stalingrad.

1943 JANUARY—Allies take Tripoli. FEBRUARY—German troops at Stalingrad surrender. APRIL—revolt of Warsaw Ghetto Jews begins. MAY—German and Italian resistance in North Africa is over; their troops surrender in Tunisia; Warsaw Ghetto revolt is put down by Germany. JULY—allies invade Sicily; Mussolini put in prison. SEPTEMBER—Allies land in Italy; Italians surrender; Germans occupy Rome; Mussolini rescued by Germany. OCTOBER—Allies capture Naples; Italy declares war on Germany. NOVEMBER—Russians recapture Kiev.

1944 JANUARY—Allies land at Anzio. JUNE—Rome falls to Allies; Allies land in Normandy (D-Day). JULY—assassination attempt on Hitler fails. AUGUST—Allies land in southern France. SEPTEMBER—Brussels freed. OCTOBER—Athens liberated. DECEMBER—Battle of the Bulge.

1945 JANUARY—Russians free Warsaw. FEBRUARY—Dresden bombed. APRIL—Americans take Belsen and Buchenwald concentration camps; Russians free Vienna; Russians take over Berlin; Mussolini killed; Hitler commits suicide. MAY—Germany surrenders; Goering captured.

THE PACIFIC THEATER

1940 SEPTEMBER—Japan joins Axis nations Germany & Italy.

1941 APRIL—Russia & Japan sign neutrality pact. DECEMBER—Japanese launch attacks against Pearl Harbor, Hong Kong, the Philippines, & Malaya; United States and Allied nations declare war on Japan; China declares war on Japan, Germany, & Italy; Japan takes over Guam, Wake Island, & Hong Kong; Japan attacks Burma.

1942 JANUARY—Japan takes over Manila; Japan invades Dutch East Indies. FEBRUARY—Japan takes over Singapore; Battle of the Java Sea. APRIL—Japanese overrun Bataan. MAY—Japan takes Mandalay; Allied forces in Philippines surrender to Japan; Japan takes Corregidor; Battle of the Coral Sea. JUNE—Battle of Midway; Japan occupies Aleutian Islands. AUGUST—United States invades Guadalcanal in the Solomon Islands.

1943 FEBRUARY—Guadalcanal taken by U.S. Marines. MARCH—Japanese begin to retreat in China. APRIL—Yamamoto shot down by U.S. Air Force. MAY—U.S. troops take Aleutian Islands back from Japan. JUNE—Allied troops land in New Guinea. NOVEMBER—U.S. Marines invade Bougainville & Tarawa.

1944 FEBRUARY—Truk liberated. JUNE—Saipan attacked by United States. JULY—battle for Guam begins. OCTOBER—U.S. troops invade Philippines; Battle of Leyte Gulf won by Allies.

1945 JANUARY—Luzon taken; Burma Road won back. MARCH—Iwo Jima freed. APRIL—Okinawa attacked by U.S. troops; President Franklin Roosevelt dies; Harry S. Truman becomes president. JUNE—United States takes Okinawa. AUGUST—atomic bomb dropped on Hiroshima; Russia declares war on Japan; atomic bomb dropped on Nagasaki. SEPTEMBER—Japan surrenders.

WORLD AT WAR

Fighter Planes

WORLD AT WAR

Fighter Planes

By R. Conrad Stein

Consultant:
Professor Robert L. Messer, Ph.D.
Department of History
University of Illinois, Chicago

CHILDRENS PRESS ®

CHICAGO

On July 1, 1940,
Goering looked
across the English
Channel toward
the British coast
in anticipation
of the long-planned
invasion of England.

FRONTISPIECE: Tension still shows in the taut lips and narrowed eyes of an American pilot who just completed a grueling seven-hour-long bomber escort mission. The writing on the back of his hand was information needed for the mission. The pilot could lick it off quickly in the event of capture by the enemy.

Library of Congress Cataloging in Publication Data

Stein, R. Conrad.
  Fighter planes.

  (World at war)
  Includes index.
  Summary: Describes the British, German, and American fighter planes used in World War II and some of the campaigns in which they played a significant part.
  1. World War, 1939-1945—Aerial operations—Juvenile literature. 2. Fighter planes—Juvenile literature. [1. World War 1939-1945—Aerial operations. 2. Fighter planes. 3. Airplanes—History] I. Title. II. Series.
D785.S84   1986   940.54′4   85-30890
ISBN 0-516-04766-3   AACR2

PICTURE CREDITS:
NATIONAL AIR AND SPACE MUSEUM: Cover, pages 4, 11 (bottom left), 14 (bottom), 16, 18, 19, 20, 21, 23, 25, 27, 28, 32, 37 (top), 38 (bottom), 39, 40, 43, 45 (bottom right), 46
LIBRARY OF CONGRESS: Page 6
VALAN PHOTOS/© ALAN WILKINSON: Page 9
PHOTRI: Pages 11 (top), 13, 17 (left), 22, 26, 38 (top), 45 (top left and right)
UPI: Pages 11 (bottom right), 12 (right), 34, 35
WIDE WORLD: Pages 12, (left), 17 (right), 24, 29, 31, 33, 36, 37 (bottom), 44, 45 (bottom left)
THE AEROPLANE: Page 14 (top)
HISTORICAL PICTURES SERVICE, INC.: Page 30

COVER PHOTO:
Before take-off, a P-51 Mustang is loaded with the ammunition for one of its six .50-caliber machine guns.

PROJECT EDITOR:
Joan Downing

CREATIVE DIRECTOR:
Margrit Fiddle

On a July morning in 1940, Hermann Goering and his staff met at a coastal town in France. Goering, the overweight chief of the German air force (Luftwaffe), peered through field glasses across the twenty-two-mile-wide English Channel toward the chalky white cliffs of Dover. The fall of France had completed Germany's lightning sweep through western Europe. Now only England, which lay across these choppy waters, stood in defiance of a complete German victory.

Setting down his field glasses, Goering smiled, waved at newsreel cameras, and then hurried away. Clearly, the Luftwaffe leader was distracted that day. Very likely, his thoughts were riveted on the coming battle against the British air force.

Earlier that year, Adolf Hitler, Goering, and the German high command had drawn plans for an invasion of England. The operation was given the code name Sea Lion. Details of the proposed invasion were sketchy and were the subject of endless debate among top officers in the German army, navy, and air force. But all the armed services agreed that the British air force had to be wiped out of the skies before Sea Lion could begin.

Goering believed he could destroy Britain's Royal Air Force (RAF) by launching massive bombing raids against targets in England. This would draw RAF fighter planes into the air, where they would have to tangle with Luftwaffe fighters. It was these buzzing, darting birds of war that would determine victory or defeat in the air war against Great Britain.

World War I open-cockpit biplanes such as the Bristol Fighter shown above could reach speeds of only seventy-five miles per hour.

By 1940, fighter planes had evolved tremendously from the open-cockpit biplanes that had engaged in wild dogfights high above the trenches of World War I. The most advanced 1940 warbirds could reach speeds in excess of 350 miles per hour and soar to the dizzying heights of thirty-six thousand feet. Compared to the kitelike fighters that had taken to the air two decades earlier, these were space-age vehicles. And German aircraft designers had machines on their drawing boards that soon would astound the world with their performances.

The principal warbirds to clash in British skies in 1940 were the Hurricanes and Spitfires of the RAF and the Messerschmitts of the Luftwaffe. The British Hawker Hurricane was an early design, and though it was dependable, it was no match for the Messerschmitt. Nevertheless, in 1940, about half the British fighter force was composed of Hurricanes, and RAF pilots were forced to rely on them. The Vickers Supermarine Spitfire and the Messerschmitt BF 109 (Me-109) were the finest fighters in Europe at the time. Even today, aviation buffs argue about which of the two was superior.

The first Spitfire rolled off a factory assembly line in 1937. Sleek and streamlined, it looked more like a racer than a military craft. A Rolls-Royce engine coupled with a trim airframe gave the plane a maximum speed of 370 miles per hour, making it faster than any other warbird in the sky. A lethal array of eight machine guns instead of the usual four made it one of the best-armed fighters in the world.

Above: At the start of the war, the British had to rely heavily on the dependable but relatively slow Hurricane.
Below: The sleek and powerful Spitfire was derived from a pre-war racing seaplane.
Left: American pilot Joe Kelly stands on the wing of his Spitfire, "Little Joe." Kelly was a member of the Eagle Squadron, a special group of Americans who flew for the RAF before the United States entered the war.

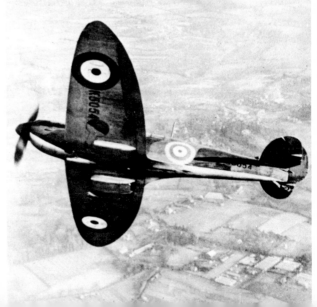

The Me-109 (above), named for its designer
Willy Messerschmitt (right), was a mainstay
of the Luftwaffe during World War II.

The German Me-109 was named for its
designer, aviation genius Willy Messerschmitt. Its
top speed was 357 miles per hour—13 miles per
hour slower than the Spitfire. However, the
Me-109 could climb faster and was able to reach
an altitude of thirty-six thousand feet, some two
thousand feet higher than the Spitfire's maximum
ceiling. Finally, the Me-109's fuel-injected engine
allowed the pilot to bank into a steep dive with no
loss of power. Engines fitted with a standard
carburetor, such as the one that powered the
Spitfire, sputtered during dives.

RAF pilots, alerted to the presence of Messerschmitt
fighters over England, scramble for their aircraft.

In July, 1940, Hermann Goering sent
squadrons of bombers accompanied by swarms of
Messerschmitt fighters into the sky above
England. The attackers were met by RAF fighters,
and what historians later called the Battle of
Britain began. Numerically, the odds favored the
Germans. At the start of the air war between the
two countries the RAF had 620 Spitfires and
Hurricanes, while the Germans were able to
launch a fighter fleet of almost 1,300 aircraft.

Over the channel and above England's green
fields the warbirds twisted, dived, and spat out
deadly hails of bullets. The fighter planes
challenged each other head-to-head at combined
speeds of more than six hundred miles per hour.

Hurricane fighters (above) twist and turn as they defend England against enemy bombers. Because the Luftwaffe pilots had to take off from bases in France (below), by the time they reached British shores they had fuel for only twenty minutes of combat.

Pilots had only two seconds to aim and fire a burst of shells from their guns. As one Spitfire pilot said, "The wicked tracers [bullets] sparkle and flash over the top of your cockpit and you break into a tight turn . . . you black out! And you ease the turn to recover in a gray unreal world of spinning horizons." Another reported going into a sudden, swift dive and then "pulling out so hard that I could feel my eyes dropping through my neck."

As the weeks of deadly combat continued, the Luftwaffe suffered stunning losses. Despite their greater numbers, German fighters labored under a number of disadvantages. The Messerschmitts had to take off from bases in France, many miles away from their targets in Britain. Because of their limited range, the Luftwaffe warbirds had fuel for only twenty minutes of combat once they reached British shores. Also, the RAF could recover British pilots who had been shot down, because they were fighting above their own soil. Once a Luftwaffe aircraft was downed, however, its crew was almost always lost or captured.

On September 7, the Luftwaffe began to "blitz" London in a series of devastating night bombing raids that lasted for more than fifty consecutive nights.

The British also used clever tactics to compensate for their weaknesses. While swift British Spitfires kept German fighters busy, the slower Hurricanes attacked German bombers. As a result, it was Hurricanes, not Spitfires, that caused the most German losses. Radar, a tool the Germans had not yet developed, gave the outnumbered British warning of German attacks. This detection system enabled the British to send their planes where they were needed most. All these factors swung the Battle of Britain to the RAF's side. The German high command was forced to cancel Operation Sea Lion. When the German bombing raids finally ceased, the once-mighty Luftwaffe had lost two thousand bombers and fighters.

American women made important contributions to the air war. Bombers produced at Douglas Aircraft in California (left) were manufactured by all-woman crews. Women Airforce Service Pilots (WASPs), commanded by famous pilot Jacqueline Cochran (right), ferried new planes from factories to American air bases.

By late 1942, large numbers of American-built warbirds began appearing over Europe. There were basic differences between these aircraft and European fighters. Hoping to produce speed, Europeans gave their fighter aircraft small, light airframes. The Americans, on the other hand, believed speed could best be attained by using powerful engines. Mightier engines meant larger fuel tanks and heavier engine mounts. The results were predictable—American fighter planes were huge compared to their European counterparts.

The massive P-47 Thunderbolt was affectionately nicknamed "the Jug."

The Republic P-47 Thunderbolt was one such massive American warbird. Its gigantic eighteen-cylinder radial engine drove a huge four-bladed propeller. When the P-47 roared down to treetop level, its thundering motor made the ground below tremble. Designers of the plane had been forced to forfeit streamlining in order to build an airframe large enough to accommodate the powerful but bulky engine. When British pilots first saw this awkward-looking aircraft, they nicknamed it "the Jug." But they were astonished by the Thunderbolt's speed. At full throttle, its mighty engine hurled it through the air at 425 miles per hour.

Above: The P-47 had to be bulky to accommodate its powerful engine, the Pratt & Whitney R-2800 Double Wasp.

Below: The latest victory of P-47 ace Warren M. Wesson is recorded by his crew chief, Clarence Koskela. Like many pilots, Wesson named his plane for his wife.

The Lockheed P-38 Lightning was a twin-engine, long-range craft.

The twin-engine Lockheed P-38 Lightning was another large American warbird. Though classified as a fighter, it outweighed many German and British light bombers. Famous for its long range, the Lightning could fly nonstop from London to Berlin and back. This allowed it to accompany bombers on their missions. Because of its great range the P-38 was particularly useful in the Pacific, where air bases were scattered over far-flung islands. Japanese pilots so respected this plane with its distinctive twin tail fins that they called it the "Fork-tailed Devil."

The sturdy bodies of American-built planes could absorb random bullet hits that knocked the more delicate German and Japanese warbirds out of the sky. The airframes of American planes were reinforced by thick steel or aluminum. Pilots were protected by armored plating fitted around the cockpits. The bulky American warbirds may have sacrificed maneuverability, but their rugged airframes carried their pilots home after sustaining damage that would have destroyed more fragile craft.

Left: In spite of serious damage to its wings and propeller, this P-47 made it home safely to its base in Italy.
Below: First Lieutenant Alva D. Henehan was nearly thrown out of the cockpit of his Thunderbolt when an exploding 88 mm shell ripped a hole large enough to stand in through the plane's right wing.

Protected by American fighter planes, B-17 Flying Fortresses (above) carried out bombing missions over Germany.

By 1943, the Americans and the British had taken the offense in the European air war. Huge fleets of bombers, some of them more than a thousand planes strong, took off from English air bases to pound targets deep in Germany. The British believed in night bombing; the Americans preferred daylight raids. Sending bombers into enemy territory during the day, however, exposed the large, slow-moving planes to attack by Germany's still-formidable fighter force. Clearly, the Americans needed long-range fighters to escort their bombers during daylight missions.

After being damaged by enemy flak, a P-38 (right) returns to its base protected by the B-17 bombers (left) it had been escorting over Bleckhammer, Germany.

Although the P-38 Lightning was a fine long-range craft, it was too big and clumsy to ward off hordes of German fighters. American bomber crews longed for a true fighter that had the range of a bomber—a combination, the experts claimed, that was impossible to achieve.

Then, in early 1944, German pilots reported clashing with a new single-engine aircraft that, miraculously, was able to escort American bombers all the way into the heart of Germany.

Luftwaffe General Adolf Galland was head of the German fighter command.

Hermann Goering refused to believe that any fighter plane could have such a range. Luftwaffe General Adolf Galland, head of the German fighter command, also doubted the reports. Deciding to see for himself if such a fantasy fighter really existed, he took to the air in a Messerschmitt to meet a formation of American bombers. The German general soon discovered that the reports were true; he was chased back to Berlin by four of the new aircraft.

The amazing American warbird that so surprised the Germans was the North American P-51 Mustang. Most aviation historians agree that this plane was the best all-around fighter of World War II.

The Mustang was a joint British-American development manufactured in America. Due to wartime necessity, the initial prototype plane was drawn up, built, and tested in only four months. The first results were less than spectacular, but when designers replaced the plane's original engine with the British-designed Rolls-Royce Merlin engine, the greatest of all warbirds was born.

The P-51 Mustang was one of the best fighter planes of World War II.

A ground crew attaches an auxiliary fuel tank to the wing
of a P-51 to give it greater range during a long mission.

By American standards, the P-51 Mustang was
a small fighter. It weighed 8,800 pounds, less than
half the weight of the twin-engine P-38 Lightning.
Yet the range of the single-engine Mustang was
remarkable. Later models of the Mustang were
able to take off from British bases, fly the width of
Germany to reach the Polish border, and return to
England—a trip covering seventeen hundred
miles. The Mustang's designers managed this
seemingly impossible range by pairing a fuel-
efficient engine with a trim airframe. Also, the
Mustang was a true fighter. In air combat, it could
maneuver as well as any fighter the Germans
could send against it. Finally, the P-51 flew at 440
miles per hour, making it one of the fastest
propeller-driven planes of the war.

Above: A ground-crew chief sits on the wing of a P-51 to guide the pilot as he taxis down the runway. The P-51's low-slung cockpit made it almost impossible for a pilot to see directly in front of him while on the ground. Below left: P-51 pilot Clarence D. "Lucky" Lester (right) discusses his latest mission. Lester, who once shot down three German planes in one mission, was a member of the distinguished all-black 332nd fighter group. Below right: P-51 pilots remove their flying clothes after returning from an escort mission over Germany.

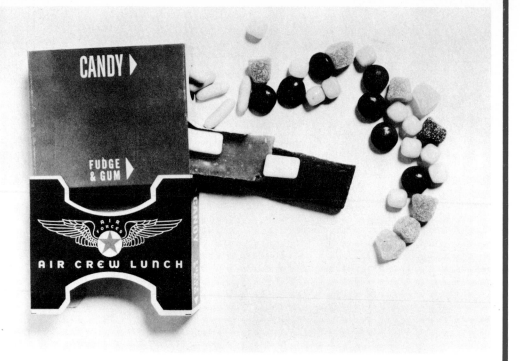

To keep up their energy during long missions, American fighter pilots were provided with an "Air Crew Lunch." It consisted of two fudge bars, assorted candy, and gum (above), and was packaged in a sliding cardboard box specially designed for one-hand operation (below).

The war in the Pacific began on December 7, 1941, when Japan launched a surprise attack on Pearl Harbor.

The air war in Europe differed from that waged over the vast Pacific Ocean. Although some of the aircraft used in the Pacific were based on land, naval planes flying from the decks of aircraft carriers took the brunt of the air combat there.

The carrier war that raged over the Pacific began on December 7, 1941, when Japanese naval aircraft struck Pearl Harbor in Hawaii. The surprise attack was made by four hundred planes that had taken off from carriers cruising many miles from the American naval base. The air raid left Pearl Harbor a shambles. Five United States battleships were sunk, and almost two hundred American planes were destroyed on the ground. The United States Navy found out at once that the Japanese naval air arm would be a formidable foe.

The leading Japanese carrier-based fighter at the start of the war was the superb Mitsubishi A6M2 *Rei-sen* (Zero Fighter). The Allies code-named this fighter Zeke, but its popular name was the Zero. American naval officers were shocked by the performance of this splendidly engineered warbird. The Zero was a compact, supremely maneuverable aircraft that could twist and turn in the sky with the grace and ease of a dancer. In level flight it reached 330 miles per hour—fast by 1941 standards—and it had an exceptionally long range. In 1941, the Zero was clearly superior to any fighter the American navy could put up against it.

The Americans put their own insignia on this captured Japanese Zero.

These Grumman Avenger torpedo bombers were among the types of aircraft escorted by carrier-based fighter planes in the Pacific.

The function of a carrier-borne fighter was essentially the same as that of a land-based fighter. The naval fighter's primary mission was to escort heavier aircraft, such as torpedo bombers, to their targets. The fighters were expected to clear the skies of enemy planes so the bombers could get through. The Japanese navy experienced a string of successes in the opening months of the war largely because the Allies had no fighter capable of outdueling the Zero.

Above: The FM-1 was an improved version of the F4F Wildcat. Right: Their wings folded, F4F Wildcats line the deck of an aircraft carrier in the Pacific.

The American navy's best fighter when the Pacific war began was the Grumman F4F Wildcat. Typically American in design, it was a large, bulky-looking plane with a powerful engine. Its blunt nose and tapering tail section led one pilot to describe the Wildcat as a "beer bottle with wings." It was a rugged vehicle, but it was slower, less maneuverable, and had a shorter range than the Zero. Wildcat pilots had to develop elaborate team tactics in order to challenge the more nimble Japanese warbirds.

The F6F Hellcat was built specifically to challenge the Japanese Zero fighter.

But Japanese naval planners erred when they failed to improve the Zero as the war dragged on. The Americans, on the other hand, kept experimenting with new fighter types. Two outstanding American naval planes that appeared later in the war were the Grumman F6F Hellcat and the Chance Vought F4U Corsair.

Commander David McCampbell, the United States Navy's leading ace pilot, called the Hellcat "the greatest plane in the war."

Remarkably, this pilot escaped with only a few scratches after crash landing what was left of his Hellcat onto his aircraft carrier.

Strangely, the Hellcat owed its design to the Zero. In the summer of 1942, American soldiers captured a Zero that had been forced to crash-land on an island near Alaska. After examining and testing the craft, American engineers built a new fighter that could outclimb and outdive it. The new plane, called the Hellcat, was one of the few American warbirds to be designed and built during the war years. Most other American fighters were evolutions of prewar designs. The Hellcat flew fifty miles per hour faster than the Zero and nearly matched it in maneuverability. In addition, it had the characteristic American-built sturdy airframe.

A ground-crew chief gives a Corsair the signal to fold its wings.

The F4U Corsair, distinguished by its upward-bending "seagull" wings, was considered a fighter-bomber rather than a pure fighter. Able to reach speeds of 420 miles per hour, it was the fastest of all American carrier-based aircraft. But it was best known for its versatility. It was a day fighter and a night fighter, a dive bomber and a reconnaissance plane, a land-based and a carrier-based fighter. It could carry two thousand-pound bombs or three auxiliary fuel tanks, and could hold eight five-inch rockets under its wings.

Major Gregory "Pappy" Boyington (first row, third from right), the top-scoring American Marine ace of the war, commanded an inexperienced but hard-fighting group of Corsair pilots nicknamed the "Black Sheep Squadron."

Led by Hellcats and Corsairs, American carrier-based planes decimated the Japanese naval air arm in a decisive battle near the Marianas Islands on June 19, 1944. In a series of frantic skirmishes, Japan lost almost three hundred planes—three fourths of its aircraft—while the United States lost only thirty. After the battle, an American pilot from the South drawled, "Heck, that was just like an old-fashioned turkey shoot." The name stuck, and the battle became known as The Great Marianas Turkey Shoot. The Japanese suffered this overwhelming defeat because they had lost most of their experienced pilots by this time and because their engineers had failed to upgrade the Zero fighter to match the new American warbirds.

Above: Soldiers on the deck of the USS *Birmingham* observe contrails
of American and Japanese fighter planes during the Great Marianas
Turkey Shoot on June 19, 1944. Below: In the aftermath of the battle,
American Marines examine a destroyed Japanese Zero fighter.

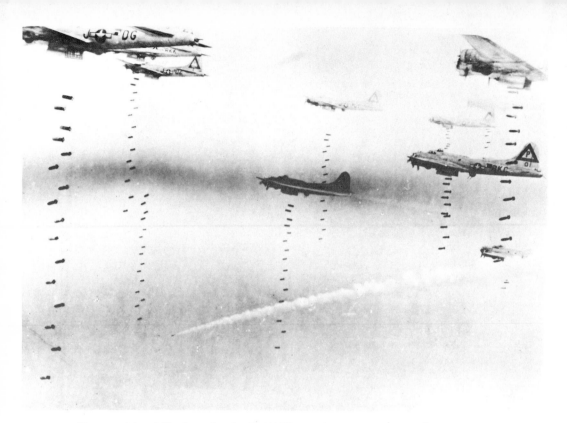

Escorted by Allied warbirds, B-17 Flying Fortresses (above) dropped
bombs (below) on Germany's cities and industrial centers in late 1944.

The German capital of Berlin was devastated by the Allied bombing raids.

Meanwhile, on the other side of the world, the Germans were flying some marvelously improved fighter types. By late 1944, Germany was covered by a cloud of Allied warplanes. Its cities and industrial centers were being devastated day and night by bombing raids. Allied command of the air was almost complete, when suddenly a revolutionary jet-powered German warbird entered the skies and changed the concept of air combat forever.

The Me-262, the world's first operational jet fighter, became
a ray of hope for the nearly defeated Luftwaffe.

The German-made Messerschmitt Me-262 was
the first operational jet aircraft to enter aerial
combat in World War II. This amazing airplane
could shoot through the clouds at the unbelievable
speed of 540 miles per hour. The few German jets
that saw combat were able to ravage Allied
bomber formations. No Allied fighter plane could
compete with them. A British pilot, after tangling
with one of the swift German jets, wrote a worried
report: "Should the enemy possess reasonable
numbers of these remarkable aircraft, it would not
be long before we lost the air superiority for which
we have struggled."

However, bickering among members of the German high command over the use of the Me-262 ultimately left the Luftwaffe without a reasonable number of the jet aircraft. In the initial development of jet power, German engineers were years ahead of the rest of the world. They had launched an experimental jet plane as early as 1939. But because Hitler, Goering, and the Luftwaffe planners enjoyed giddying success at the beginning of the war, they showed little interest in perfecting a practical jet warplane. Later, Hitler insisted that jets be used to propel bombers so the Luftwaffe could retake the offensive. Finally, the German leader approved the production of a jet fighter, but his dawdling had slowed the growth of what could have been the Luftwaffe's wonder weapon. By the time the Me-262 jets were being produced in significant numbers, Germany was already at the mercy of her enemies.

The Luftwaffe had other aircraft with advanced designs that they hoped to use in a last-ditch battle against the Allies. One was the Messerschmitt 163B Komet, a tiny rocket-powered fighter plane that reached speeds of six hundred miles per hour. The Germans also built a bizarre, conventionally powered fighter that had a second engine and a propeller mounted on the tail. Able to reach speeds of 470 miles per hour, it was one of the fastest piston-driven aircraft ever built. In the war's closing weeks, the Luftwaffe operated the Heinkel He-162, a fighter plane powered by a jet engine but built with an airframe made of cheap, lightweight plywood. Although these aircraft were cleverly engineered, they were produced too late to be a factor in the air war.

The tailless Me-163B Komet (above) was the first rocket-powered plane to be used in combat. The Heinkel He-162, also a jet fighter, was called the "People's Fighter" because its body was made of cheap plywood. Both planes came along too late to make a difference in the outcome of the war.

Finally, it must be remembered that the fighter war over Europe and the Pacific was more than a clash between opposing machines. The warbirds were flown by men who experienced the same terrors felt by soldiers and sailors. Fighter pilots on both sides of the conflict had to be intelligent and physically fit. Thousands of these young men, the best the warring nations could offer, were killed, wounded, or horribly burned during the long years of air combat. Prime Minister Winston Churchill expressed his nation's gratitude to the fighter pilots who fought the Battle of Britain when he said, "Never in the field of human conflict was so much owed by so many to so few."

Britain's Prime Minister Winston Churchill

Some of the famous fighter aces of World War II were Richard Bong (above left), who shot down forty enemy planes to become the war's highest-scoring American ace; Thomas McGuire (above right), who with thirty-eight victories was the second-best American ace; British pilot John E. Johnson (below left), a leading ace in the European air war; and David McCampbell (below right), the United States Navy's highest scorer.

Wildcats in the Pacific return home after a long
day of offensive action against the enemy.

Index

Page numbers in boldface type indicate illustrations

About the Author

Mr. Stein was born and grew up in Chicago. At eighteen he enlisted in the Marine Corps where he served three years. He was a sergeant at discharge. He later received a B.A. in history from the University of Illinois and an M.F.A. from the University of Guanajuato in Mexico.

Although he served in the Marines, Mr. Stein believes that wars are a dreadful waste of human life. He agrees with a statement once uttered by Benjamin Franklin: "There never was a good war or a bad peace." But wars are all too much a part of human history. Mr. Stein hopes that some day there will be no more wars to write about.